OCT   2013

EDGE BOOKS™

WILD ABOUT SNAKES

COPPERHEADS

BY MELANIE A. HOWARD

Consultants:
Joe Maierhauser, President/CEO
Terry Phillip, Curator of Reptiles
Reptile Gardens
Rapid City, South Dakota

CAPSTONE PRESS
a capstone imprint

Edge Books are published by Capstone Press,
1710 Roe Crest Drive, North Mankato, Minnesota 56003.
www.capstonepub.com

Books published by Capstone Press are manufactured with paper
containing at least 10 percent post-consumer waste.

Library of Congress Cataloging-in-Publication Data
Howard, Melanie A.
   Copperheads / by Melanie A. Howard.
      p. cm. — (Edge books: wild about snakes)
   Includes bibliographical references and index.
   ISBN 978-1-4296-7663-2 (library binding)
   ISBN 978-1-4296-8017-2 (paperback)
   1. Copperhead—Juvenile literature. I. Title.
   QL666.O69H69 2012
   597.96'3—dc23   2011021019

Editorial Credits
Brenda Haugen, editor; Gene Bentdahl, designer; Laura Manthe,
   production specialist

Photo Credits
Alamy: Photoshot Holdings Ltd, 7; Corbis: Joe McDonald, 8, 21, 22;
Dreamstime: James Deboer, cover, Mgkuijpers, 1, Outdoorsman, 10; fotolia:
Brandy McKnight, 24-25; Getty Images: National Geographic/George Grail,
16-17, Visuals Unlimited/Jim Merli, 18-19, Visuals Unlimited/Joe McDonald,
14-15; Photo Researchers, Inc: Suzanne L. & Joseph T. Collins, 12; Photolibrary:
Peter Arnold/James Gerholdt, 11; photoshot holdings: Joe McDonald, 27;
Shutterstock: Jason Patrick Ross, 5, 29; U.S. Fish and Wildlife Service, 13

Artistic Effects
Shutterstock: Marilyn Volan

Printed in the United States of America in Stevens Point, Wisconsin.
102011   006404WZS12

TABLE OF CONTENTS

Chapter 1

SNAKE-MEN

A Cherokee Indian legend explains why copperheads and people don't always get along. The legend says that there was a time when the Sun hated people. Every day the Sun would go to visit her daughter. When she got close to her daughter's house, she sent down rays so hot that people started dying. The Cherokee were afraid of the Sun and went to the Little Men for help. The Little Men were people who could make medicine and perform miracles. The Little Men told the Cherokee the only way to stop the Sun was to kill her.

The Little Men changed two Cherokee men into snakes. One became a black hognose snake and the other a copperhead. The two snakes waited along the path the Sun took to visit her daughter. They planned to bite the Sun and kill her with **venom**.

When the Sun got close, the hognose snake jumped out to bite. But he was blinded by the Sun's light and could spit out only yellow slime. The Sun just gave the hognose snake a dirty look and went into her daughter's house unharmed. The copperhead didn't do anything. It just slithered away. In time the Cherokee and the Sun made peace. But the cowardly copperhead was never loved by the people.

Not all stories about copperheads are old legends. Today a popular story about copperheads circulates through e-mail. The story involves baby copperheads being found in the lining of a flowerpot, but it isn't true.

venom—a poisonous liquid produced by some animals

Close Encounters

Copperheads aren't always loved by people today either. Many people fear a copperhead's venomous bite. A copperhead is a pit viper. Pit vipers are a group of snakes that find **prey** using heat-seeking pits on the sides of their faces. But copperheads aren't as deadly as other pit vipers such as the rattlesnake. People rarely die from copperhead bites.

Copperheads live in the eastern United States and northeastern Mexico. They make their home in many **habitats**. They are found in woodlands, ravines, swamps, fields, grasslands, streams, and rocky hillsides. They also live in empty buildings and under trash piles in cities. Copperheads have even been found in people's basements.

Since they live so close together, it's no wonder people and copperheads keep running into one another. The meetings often do not end well. Many snakes get killed when they are found because people are afraid of the copperhead's bite.

prey—an animal hunted by another animal for food
habitat—the natural place and conditions in which an animal or plant lives

Copperhead Range

☐ where copperheads live

North America

South America

Europe

Asia

Africa

Australia

Antarctica

N
W • E
S

Pit Vipers

Pit vipers are unique snakes. They have hinged fangs as other vipers do. But they also have heat-sensing pits on both sides of their faces. The pits allow them to find and track their prey's body heat. One kind of pit viper, the rattlesnake, has evolved to include a rattle on its tail. The rattle warns enemies to stay away.

Chapter 2

BLENDING IN

Copperheads have body markings that help
them blend in with their surroundings. The
markings vary in color from bright orange-red
to nearly black. Most copperheads are
red-brown with copper-colored heads.
Copperheads are named for this color pattern.

How can you tell a copperhead from other types of snakes? Copperheads have hourglass markings along their backs and triangle-shaped heads. A thin line on either side of the snake's head goes straight through its eyes. Copperheads have slit-shaped **pupils**.

Scary Similarities

Several harmless snakes, such as the milk snake, look like copperheads. Milk snakes have banded hourglass markings and often come in the same colors as copperheads. Milk snakes' heads are narrower, but it is still easy to mistake a milk snake for a copperhead. The similarities scare some people into killing milk snakes. If you see a snake and cannot tell what kind it is from a safe distance, don't go any closer. Call your local fish and wildlife organization and ask to have the snake removed. Even if the snake turns out to be harmless, it is better to be safe than sorry.

pupil–the round, dark center of the eye that lets in light

Types of Copperheads

There are five types of copperhead snakes. The northern copperhead lives in Massachusetts, Illinois, Alabama, and Georgia. It's between 22 and 53 inches (56 and 135 centimeters) long. The hourglass shapes on the back of northern copperheads have dark outlines. Spots often are found between the hourglass shapes. The northern copperhead is **endangered** in Massachusetts.

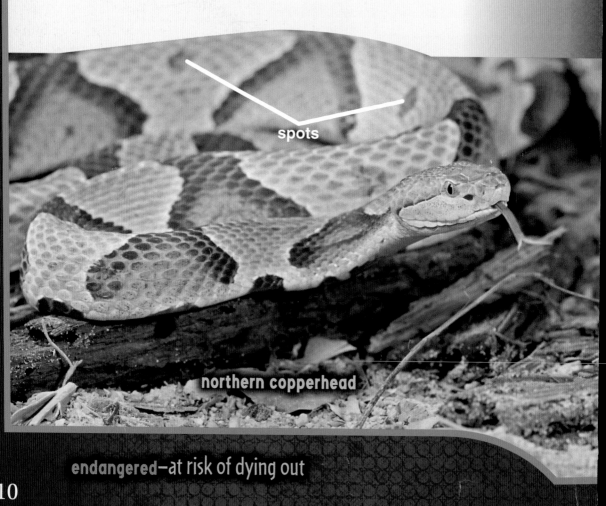

spots

northern copperhead

endangered—at risk of dying out

southern copperhead

The southern copperhead is between 24 and 36 inches (61 and 90 cm) long. It lives between southern North Carolina and southern Missouri. Its range reaches south to northern Florida. Southern copperheads have hourglass shapes on their backs that often come together sharply in the middle. Sometimes the hourglass shapes are broken at the middle and the two halves do not meet. The hourglass shapes are often outlined in white. Southern copperheads' bodies are usually brown.

Osage copperheads are usually between 24 and 36 inches (61 and 90 cm) long. The Osage copperhead looks a lot like the northern copperhead. But Osage copperheads have darker bands outlining the hourglass shapes on their backs, and they don't have spots. The Osage copperhead has a gray- or black-marked, marble-patterned belly. Osage copperheads live in Illinois, Iowa, Missouri, Nebraska, Kansas, and Oklahoma.

Osage copperhead

broad-banded copperhead

The broad-banded copperhead gets its name from the thick, red bands along its back. These bands are so wide, they look more like stripes than the hourglass pattern. The broad-banded copperhead is smaller than most copperheads. It is between 22 and 30 inches (56 and 76 cm) long. The broad-banded copperhead lives in Oklahoma and Texas.

During the U.S. Civil War (1861–1865), northerners who wanted to make peace with the South were called copperheads. Calling someone a copperhead was meant as an insult.

The smallest but most colorful of the copperheads is the Trans-Pecos copperhead. It is between 20 and 30 inches (51 and 76 cm) long. The Trans-Pecos copperhead varies in color from chestnut brown to dark orange. The snake's belly is light orange with red bands. The hourglass bands on its back are outlined in white. There is also a thin white outline on the sides of its face. Trans-Pecos copperheads live in Texas and in the states of Coahuila and Chihuahua in Mexico.

The average height of an American male is 5 feet, 10 inches (178 centimeters).

Trans-Pecos copperhead

northern copperhead

Trans-Pecos copperhead

Same Name, Different Families

The most well-known copperheads are probably the copperheads found in North America. But two other snakes from different families share that name. Both are also known for their coppery or red color.

Australian copperheads are venomous snakes that belong to the cobra family. They live along the southern coast of Australia and on Tasmania, an island off Australia's southeastern coast. The copperheads of India are also known as radiated rat snakes. They belong to the rat snake family and are not venomous.

Chapter 3

MATING AND HUNTING

Copperheads can sometimes be found near other snakes. Copperheads **hibernate** with other copperheads, rattlesnakes, black racers, and rat snakes during the winter. But copperheads will fight each other during mating season in late spring and early fall.

Male copperheads compete for females during mating season. During a fight, copperheads lift their bodies up and sway side to side. Then they hook necks. They sometimes wrap their whole bodies around each other. The males then try to pin each other to the ground. The male that wins the fight gets to mate with the female.

hibernate—to spend winter in a deep sleep

Staying Warm

Copperheads like to bask in the sun. By lying in the sun, they warm themselves. Snakes try to keep their bodies at a certain temperature so that they can move, hunt, and even digest their food better. If it gets too hot or too cold, a snake can lose its ability to move well. It could even die.

Copperhead, the Villain

Some copperhead traits have inspired characters in comics. Copperhead was a villain in DC Comics. He first appeared in the Batman comic *The Brave and the Bold* #78 in June 1968. In that comic, Copperhead fought Batman and Wonder Woman. Copperhead was a clever thief. Though he was human, Copperhead could squeeze and kill people with the tail of his suit.

Later, Copperhead made a deal with a demon to become a living snake-man who spit venom. He used his new powers to become an assassin. In 2004 Copperhead was killed by Kate Spencer in the comic *Manhunter* #1.

Young Copperheads

Female copperheads give birth to between one and 17 live young during the summer. At birth the young snakes are encased in sacks, but they quickly break free. Giving birth to live young instead of laying eggs helps protect young copperheads from **predators** that eat eggs.

Copperheads are born with **fangs** and venom. Young copperheads have brighter tail tips than adult copperheads. Baby copperheads lie in wait and use their brightly-colored tails as lures. Their bright tails make curious prey come closer. Then the young copperhead can strike.

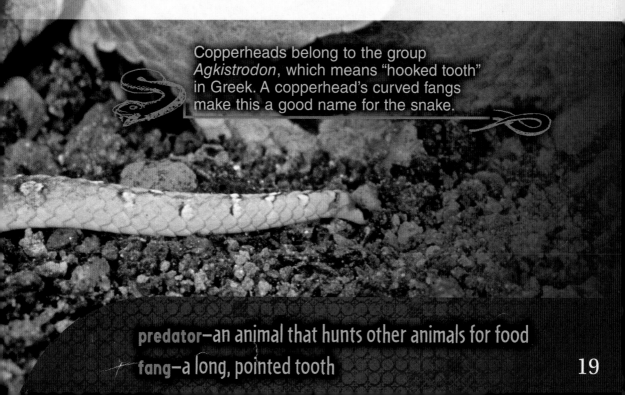

Copperheads belong to the group *Agkistrodon*, which means "hooked tooth" in Greek. A copperhead's curved fangs make this a good name for the snake.

predator—an animal that hunts other animals for food
fang—a long, pointed tooth

Lying in Wait

An adult copperhead often lies in wait and ambushes its prey as it comes near. A copperhead may hide in the same spot for days, waiting for prey. Using its heat-sensing pits and its good sense of smell, a copperhead can sense prey even at night. Then it strikes a passing animal. During the summer, copperheads are most active at night. At other times of the year, copperheads are more active at twilight. They are especially active after rainfall.

What's that Smell?

Like other snakes, copperheads smell using a Jacobson's organ. A snake flicks its tongue in and out as it gathers air molecules and pulls them into its mouth. Then the snake sticks the fork of its tongue into small holes at the top of its mouth. This is where the Jacobson's organ is. Using this organ, the snake's brain can decode the smell.

ambush—to attack by surprise
twilight—the time of day when the sun has just set and it's beginning to get dark

Copperheads only need to eat 10 or 12 times a year, depending on how big the meals are.

Not Picky Eaters

Not all snakes eat **warm-blooded** and **cold-blooded** prey, but copperheads do. Mice are a common meal for an adult copperhead. Adult copperheads also eat small birds, lizards, and small snakes. Young copperheads eat caterpillars and other insects. Like all snakes, copperheads can swallow prey wider than their own bodies. Copperheads' flexible jaws allow their mouths to stretch.

A copperhead relies on its venom to kill its prey. A copperhead's hinged fangs fold out from the roof of its mouth when it is time to strike. Each time a copperhead strikes, the snake injects a small amount of venom into its prey. A copperhead's venom breaks down the prey's red blood cells, killing the animal. Once the prey is dead—or at least stops moving— the copperhead swallows it whole. Powerful juices in a copperhead's stomach break down the prey's body—even its bones.

warm-blooded—having a body temperature that stays about the same all the time

cold-blooded—having a body temperature that changes with the surroundings

Chapter 4

COPPERHEADS AND PEOPLE

Unlike other snakes, copperheads have adapted well to people changing their habitat. But people do pose a big threat to copperheads. People often kill copperheads when the snakes are found in homes or near places where people work and live.

Many snakes are also killed on roads. Sometimes people purposely kill snakes on the road. Scientists believe this is because many people are afraid of snakes. Their fear causes them to react violently toward the snakes.

 After summer rainstorms, copperheads often lie out on warm, wet roads.

Warning Sign

When a person stumbles upon a copperhead, the snake is unpredictable. Sometimes a copperhead will strike right away. It might even strike more than once. At other times, the snake will just try to escape.

A copperhead that feels threatened will often beat its tail around the leaves and brush around it. A copperhead will shake its tail much like a rattlesnake does, though copperheads don't have rattles. Still, copperheads can make quite a racket by beating the leaves and brush.

Copperheads bite more people in the United States every year than any other snake. Even though the bites rarely cause deaths, copperhead bites should be taken seriously. A person who has been bitten by a copperhead should be taken to the hospital right away.

Snake Medicine

Though they are not well-liked, copperheads play an important part in nature. Like most snakes, copperheads keep the **rodent** population down. Rodents can carry diseases that are harmful to people. Also, southern copperhead venom has been studied. It could one day help fight cancer or other diseases. Given the great work they do for us, it might be time for people to give copperheads a second chance.

rodent—a mammal with long front teeth used for gnawing; rats, mice, and squirrels are rodents

A Treatment for Cancer?

The chemical in southern copperhead venom that scientists study is called contortrostatin (kon-TOHR-troh-stat-in). Often cancer will start in one place in a person's body and then spread to another place.

Contortrostatin helps stop cancer from spreading through a person's body. The chemical binds to the part of the cancer cell that allows it to stick itself to other places in the body. This keeps the cancer from being able to stick elsewhere. Contortrostatin has also shown it can stop cancer cells from sticking to each other.

GLOSSARY

ambush (AM-bush)—to attack by surprise

cold-blooded (KOHLD-BLUH-duhd)—having a body temperature that changes with the surroundings

endangered (in-DAYN-juhrd)—at risk of dying out

fang (FANG)—a long, pointed tooth

habitat (HAB-uh-tat)—the natural place and conditions in which an animal or plant lives

hibernate (HYE-bur-nate)—to spend winter in a deep sleep

predator (PRED-uh-tur)—an animal that hunts other animals for food

prey (PRAY)—an animal hunted by another animal for food

pupil (PYOO-puhl)—the round, dark center of the eye that lets in light

rodent (ROHD-uhnt)—a mammal with long front teeth used for gnawing; rats, mice, and squirrels are rodents

twilight (TWYE-lyte)—the time of day when the sun has just set and it's beginning to get dark

venom (VEN-uhm)—a poisonous liquid produced by some animals

warm-blooded (WOHRM-BLUH-duhd)—having a body temperature that stays about the same all the time

READ MORE

Green, Jen. *Snakes*. Amazing Animal Hunters. Mankato, Minn.: Amicus, 2011.

Jackson, Tom. *Deadly Snakes*. Dangerous Animals. New York: Gareth Stevens Pub., 2011.

Taylor, Barbara. *100 Things You Should Know about Snakes*. Broomall, Penn.: Mason Crest, 2011.

INTERNET SITES

FactHound offers a safe, fun way to find Internet sites related to this book. All of the sites on FactHound have been researched by our staff.

Here's all you do:

Visit *www.facthound.com*

Type in this code: 9781429676632

INDEX